Other books by Ingri & Edgar Parin d'Aulaire

ABRAHAM LINCOLN

BENJAMIN FRANKLIN

BUFFALO BILL

COLUMBUS

GEORGE WASHINGTON

LEIF THE LUCKY

*The drawings for this book were lithographed directly on stone by the artists
and lithographed in four colors in the United States of America.*

POCAHONTAS

ISBN 0-9643803-6-6

Published by Beautiful Feet Books
139 Main Street
Sandwich, MA 02563

www.bfbooks.com
508-833-8626

POCAHONTAS

INGRI & EDGAR PARIN D'AULAIRE

BEAUTIFUL FEET BOOKS

In the year 1607
the first Englishmen came
sailing across the ocean to settle the part of
the new world which they called Virginia after their
virgin queen Elizabeth. They might all have perished
if it had not been for the help they got from
the Indian Princess Pocahontas.
This is her story.

In the dark woods of Virginia, where dusky owls hooted over the treetops and prowling beasts howled at the moon,

there lived a stern old Indian chief. His name was Powhatan, and he ruled over thirty tribes.

He had a little daughter who was the very apple of his eye. She was as sweet and pretty as he was ugly and cruel.

He gave her the finest feathers and the shiniest shells when he came home from the warpath, for he was so very fond of her.

"Oh, that little one is sweet, but full of pranks, and only wants to play," said the squaws. They worked from morning till night and their girls had to help them. But the mighty Powhatan's dearest daughter was allowed to skip and dance.

He gave her the name Pocahontas, which means the one who plays mostly.

Ingri Edgar

While the shadows were long and the woods around were black, Pocahontas slept snugly in her father's longhouse. But at the dawn of day she jumped from her bed mat, ran out the door and down to the bank of the river. Warm or cold, summer or winter, she took her morning bath every day, for that would make her healthy and strong.

When the sun rose she stood on the bank and beamed toward the sun and sang a small song in its honor. Round and red the sun beamed back. With a splash she jumped into the water.

After her swim she tied a deerskin around her waist and some beads around her neck.

Now Pocahontas could run and play with the boys. But the other girls must go home to help the squaws cook and garden.

14

Pocahontas ran and frolicked in the woods and fair meadows. She grew strong and straight and supple as a cat, and could find her way in the deepest forest. There she gathered berries and herbs and brought them to her grandmother's hut.

Grandmother was so old and frail that she sat in the smoke by her fire and shivered and froze. But there was no end to all that she knew! She made healing drinks and ointments from the berries and herbs that Pocahontas brought. She made pots of clay and mats of sweet-smelling grass. With sharp flint she cut clothes from deerskin.

While she worked she talked and mumbled. She was full of stories and magic.

16

She told Pocahontas about the Great Spirit the Indians worshiped, and about the other spirits that lived in the sun, in trees, in rocks, and even in animals. Some of the spirits were good. They watched over the Indians. Pocahontas must never forget to praise the good spirits. But there were other spirits that were mischievous and even very wicked. Gentle words might keep them from doing harm. Oh, it was much that Grandmother knew.

In all the world there was only one who knew still more about spirits and magic than Grandmother, thought Pocahontas. That was Powhatan's medicine man. He knew secret magic ways to find answers to every question.

Then one day white men came to Powhatan's land. Their like the Indians had never seen. On huge boats they were blown straight in from the great waters. From their boats roared the voice of thunder itself. At once they began to build a village in Powhatan's land. They chopped down his trees, they hunted his game, and acted as though they owned his land. They were not afraid of offending Powhatan even though he was so mighty that everyone trembled when he frowned.

They must be dangerous sorcerers, Powhatan's people thought. It wasn't only that they did not look like regular people with their pale faces and their hair like corn silk. But in their hands they carried magic sticks that spat fire which killed whatever it hit.

Yes, they were so dangerous and full of sorcery that even Powhatan did not go against them quickly with all his braves to chase them out of his land. His medicine man sat at his side and juggled and conjured to try to find out what kind of magic the palefaces practiced, but he could not make it out.

All that summer the Indians worried and wondered, and the children cried and went into hiding when anybody said "Paleface."

One day Pocahontas sat in the garden, playing with a doll she had made of a corncob. Suddenly she laughed right out loud! The palefaces looked just like her corncob doll.

Then she was certain their magic could not be evil, for corn was the Indian's best friend.

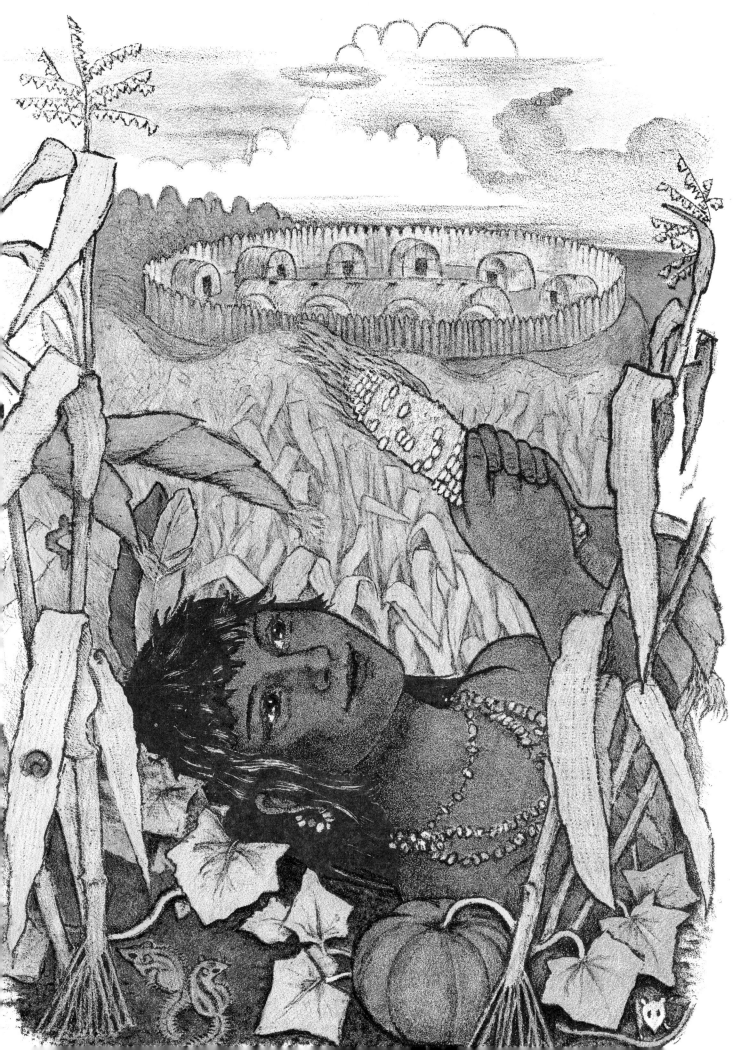

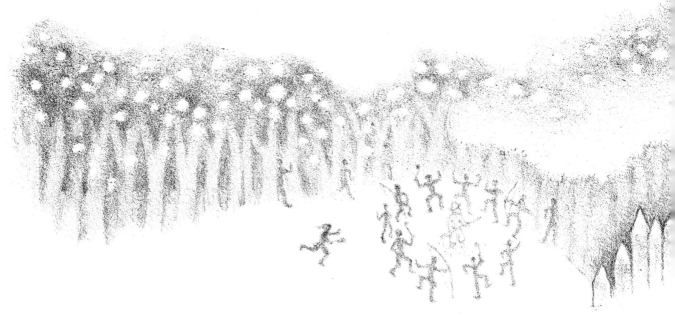

When fall came the Indians captured one of the white leaders. He had ventured too far away from the white men's village and a band of Indian warriors caught him in a swamp. They dragged him through the woods to Powhatan's village, so the mighty chief himself could decide what should be done with him.

Powhatan called his medicine man and the medicine man called his helpers. They painted their faces in the most awesome manner with green and red and black paint, and the medicine man adorned his head with stuffed snakes and weasels.

When the prisoner was brought into the village the children yelled. But Pocahontas was not the least bit afraid. She thought he was the handsomest man she had ever seen. His eyes were strange and blue as the sky, but she could see no evil in them.

She painted her face a glowing red and hurried into her ceremonial robe of white turkey feathers, so she could take her place beside her father when he judged the prisoner.

He was an English captain and his name was John Smith. He was the hardiest and shrewdest of the white men who had come to Powhatan's land.

In Powhatan's longhouse John Smith faced the chief bravely. With
words and with signs he answered all questions outright. Powhatan looked pleased with what he heard. "My father
will let him live," thought Pocahontas. But
the medicine men were scowling as
they danced and shouted and
worked their magic.

INGRI

At last they spoke to Powhatan, and said that the spirits had told them the white man's magic was evil, the prisoner must die. But as the medicine men made ready to kill John Smith, Pocahontas suddenly rushed forward. She took his head in her arms and laid her head upon his to save him from death.

The medicine men grumbled but Powhatan said the prisoner should live. For there was a custom among the Indians that a maiden could save a prisoner from death if she had taken a liking to him. Then he was her property.

So the English captain and the little Indian princess became fast friends. He whittled dolls and toys for her with his sharp knife of steel and showed her some of his things, which the Indians thought were magic.

In his big pocket he had many strange things. There was a little spirit that lived in a box. The spirit always pointed straight to the north. With it John Smith could never get lost in the thickest woods. It really was a compass, but to Pocahontas it was magic.

He told about his country, England, far away on the other side of the sea, and about his chief, who was the King of England. This king was still mightier than Powhatan. His house of snow-white stone was as large as a whole Indian village. There, little princesses ran about clad in silk and silver and gold and played with pearls and diamonds.

Of more and more wondrous things he talked, until even Powhatan was so impressed that he called John Smith his son and said if he wanted he might return to the white men's village.

So John Smith bade good-by to his little Indian princess and said: "My princess jewel, bring me your little basket and I will fill it with blue beads."

The other Indian girls all envied Pocahontas her beautiful beads. But to her nothing seemed much fun after her white friend had left. When she heard that John Smith and his people were sick and hungry in their village, she begged and prayed till her father let her go to them with food. She filled great baskets with corn and asked her playmates to help her carry them. Leading the procession through the woods, she trudged the long way to Jamestown, the white men's village.

The white men had not provided for winter and now they were sick and hungry. They wept and lamented and wanted to leave the dreary land to which they had come. For all that he tried, John Smith could not cheer them up.

He thanked and praised Pocahontas when she came with all the corn, for when his men had eaten their fill they cheered up. Pocahontas was so happy to see John Smith again that she stood on her head and turned somersaults.

Many times that winter Pocahontas came with food for the Jamestown settlers. Her father let her go, but he was not too pleased.

Powhatan liked it still less when John Smith and his men came sailing straight up the river to his village to buy corn.

Gruffly he sold them a little, but he made them pay a very high price. When, soon afterward, they came sailing again in their ships, he flatly refused to see them. But John Smith sent a message to him that this time he did not come for corn but to bring rare gifts from the King of England himself.

For when King James of England had heard of the mighty Powhatan who ruled over thirty tribes, he said:

"Why, he is a king and an emperor and my royal brother! Royal gifts must be taken to him, and a crown must be put upon his head."

So Powhatan received the English.

They brought a huge bed into his longhouse.

"That is from your royal brother the King of England," they said.

They carried in a shiny basin and pitcher.

"These are from your royal brother the King of England," they said.

They hung a purple cape over his shoulders.

"This is from your royal brother the King of England," they said.

Powhatan was mighty pleased, and gave them his shaggy coonskin robe as a present for their king.

But when they wanted Powhatan to kneel so they could put the crown upon his head he refused. For Powhatan had never stooped for anyone. Crowned he must be, for the King of England had ordered it. So they pushed and pulled till they made him bend just a little, and quickly they put the crown upon his head. This done, the English gave a sign to their ships on the river, and the ships answered with a thundering salute from all their guns. Powhatan jumped up in alarm, but the English quickly assured him that the thunder was all in his honor.

After that Powhatan was in great good humor and had a feast prepared for the Englishmen. They were led out into a fair meadow and asked to sit down around a fire.

There they sat, toasting their toes, when suddenly they heard loud shouts and shrieks from the woods. Now it was the English who jumped up in alarm, but they sat down again quickly.

Out from the trees whirled Pocahontas, leading a band of young girls. The girls were painted in gleaming colors and each had a pair of antlers tied to her head. Leaping and yelling, they stormed up to the fire, and danced an Indian dance around it. As suddenly as they had come, they ran back into the woods. There they took off their antlers and paint, and gently walked back to the meadow.

Now the Indians led the white men to the house where the food was prepared, and they made merry and feasted together. They ate corn and fish, turkey and venison, and pumpkin and berries till far into the night.

Next day they parted as friends.

By spring the Indians themselves had little food left and were hungry and cross. Then John Smith came sailing again for the third time. He threatened and thundered that his people must have corn, and he would not take no for an answer.

This made Powhatan so angry that he decided to make an end to John Smith and his men. But the cunning old chief hid his wrath and calmly told the Englishmen to spend the night in a house off in the woods. He planned to come with his braves and do away with them while they slept.

But once more Pocahontas saved John Smith's life.

She did not want to take sides against her father, but she could not let him kill her white friend. She wept and wrung her hands and did not know what to do. But in the dark of night she slipped quietly through the woods and warned John Smith not to go to sleep. He wanted to reward her with pretty beads, but with tears in her eyes she refused.

John Smith and his men got away safely. But after that there were no more signs of friendship between the red men and the white men. They fought and took from each other whatever they could. Pocahontas was not allowed to go to Jamestown to see John Smith any more.

Later she heard that he was hurt when his gunpowder blew up. Dying or dead he had been carried aboard a ship that sailed for England.

A few years passed and Pocahontas grew to a beautiful maiden. She had many suitors, but she turned them all down and her father was not pleased with her.

One day he sent her on an errand to a village far away. There she was the guest of the village chief and his wife. They were ugly and cruel people.

An English sea captain sailed his ship up to the village. When he saw Pocahontas there he thought: "I'll kidnap her and in exchange for her Powhatan will be sure to give us back all he has taken from us." So he promised the village chief and his wife a shiny copper kettle if they would help him.

The wife made a fuss and pretended she would never be happy again if she could not go aboard the ship. But her husband would not take her unless Pocahontas went with her. Pocahontas did not want to go, but the wife carried on till Pocahontas came with her. Then the captain used sweet words and lured Pocahontas to the gun room, to show her where the thunder was made.

While she was there the chief and his wife grabbed the copper kettle and hurriedly paddled off without her.

Pocahontas wept and begged to be put ashore. But to no avail. The sea captain pulled up his anchor, hoisted his sail, and took her away to Jamestown.

Thus was the Princess Pocahontas sold for a copper kettle.

In Jamestown her friends were kind to her and did what they could to cheer her up while they waited for her father to buy her free. But Powhatan fooled them. He would give back to the Englishmen only half of what they asked for his daughter.

Among her friends in Jamestown there was a young man whose name was John Rolfe. He grew so fond of her that he felt he could not live without her. While she sat there and wept and sorrowed that her father would not buy her back, John Rolfe came to her and said he would give her all that he had in the world and always be kind to her if she would marry him. Yes, maybe some day he would even take her to England.

She gave him her hand and vowed to marry him if her father said yes.

That he did.

So Pocahontas was christened and named Rebecca, for she must also have a Christian name.

Then they had the wedding in Jamestown and made merry and feasted for many days. Powhatan did not come to her wedding, for never would the mighty chief set foot in the white men's village. But many of her friends and relatives came.

Both the Indians and the English were pleased with the wedding. They hoped that with Powhatan's dearest daughter married to an Englishman there would be no more wars between the white and the red men in Powhatan's land.

When some time had passed Pocahontas had a little boy child. He was pinker than a white child and paler than an Indian child. The Indians said: "Oh, he will be darker when he grows up." The white people said: "Oh, he will be fairer when he grows up." But to Pocahontas he was the most beautiful child in the whole world.

It was told about in England that one of the Jamestown settlers had married an Indian princess. Everyone who heard about her wanted to see what she looked like. Soon it was decided that John Rolfe should take his family to England for a visit.

Oh, how happy Pocahontas was. Now she would see for herself the wondrous things that John Smith had told her about.

Powhatan, too, was pleased, for he would like to find out how mighty England was and what kind of man his royal brother the King of England might be. He sent one of his most trusted braves with his daughter, for he thought that four eyes would see more than two.

So Pocahontas and her family and train of attendants sailed off across the great waters. They sailed for days and they sailed for weeks and they sailed for months. At last they came to an English port.

As soon as they landed Powhatan's trusted brave started to notch away on a stick he had brought with him. For Powhatan had given him a sheaf of sticks and told him to make a notch for every Englishman he saw so he would know how many men the King of England had.

The Indian notched and notched, but the faster he notched the more people popped up. It was the deuce how many men there were in England.

From the port they traveled on. At last they came to London itself.
Pocahontas could hardly believe her own eyes, for across the huge river
stood London Bridge, and on top of the bridge were built houses as high
as the tallest trees in the forest at home. All of a sudden a span of the bridge

swung open, and there, far up the river, lay the King's snow-white palace glistening in the sun. White swans swam on the river, and all around were wondrous gardens with beautiful flowers and strange fruits. Fine ladies and gentlemen, all dressed in shimmering silks, walked about.

So Pocahontas came into the turmoil of Londontown. There was a din of carriage wheels and horses' hoofs and the voices of thousands of people. Powhatan's brave glanced around. Then, with a grunt, he threw the sticks away. Powhatan would never believe there could be so many people in all the world as he saw there in London.

Much ado was made of Pocahontas. Great ladies opened their doors to her. They gave balls and banquets in her honor and took her to the theater to see plays written by William Shakespeare. Artists painted her portrait. Poets wrote songs in her honor. Her name was on everyone's lips.

Then one day, whom should Pocahontas see but John Smith. There he stood among all the strangers, for the skillful doctors in England had healed his serious wounds. He bowed low before Pocahontas and called her Lady Rebecca. He had not forgotten his little Indian friend who had become so lovely a lady.

He wrote a letter to the Queen of England and told her all that Pocahontas had done for him and the other Jamestown settlers. Without her help many Englishmen would have died of hunger. And so the Queen of England herself invited the Princess Pocahontas to come to her palace.

The Queen showed her much honor and everybody admired the beautiful Virginia princess. Perhaps, if they had seen her running about in the woods, barefoot and dressed only in a skin, they would not have thought her so much of a princess.

And as for Pocahontas, when she bowed before the King and saw the skinny legs that could hardly carry the fat body of the King of England, she thought of her stately father. He needed neither a crown on his head nor a scepter in his hand to show that he was a ruler.

She held her head as high as though she had been born in a snow-white palace. She was proud of being her father's daughter and of having been born in a hut of bark in the midst of the deep, dark woods of Virginia. Pocahontas herself never returned to her home across the great water. But Powhatan's brave and the other Indians went back, and told such tall tales of the wonders of England that nobody would believe them. And when Pocahontas's son was a grown man, he sailed to his mother's country. There he became the father of a great, big family which lives on to this very day.